THE GREEN ZONE CONVERSATION BOOK

by the same author

THE CONVERSATION TRAIN

**A Visual Approach to Conversation for
Children on the Autism Spectrum**
ISBN 978 1 84905 986 2 (US and Canada)
eISBN 978 0 85700 900 5
ISBN 978 1 84905 531 4 (UK and rest of world)
eISBN 978 0 85700 954 8

of related interest

TALK TO ME

**Conversation Strategies for Parents of
Children on the Autism Spectrum or with
Speech and Language Impairments**
Heather Jones
ISBN 978 1 84905 428 7
eISBN 978 0 85700 898 5

FINDING COMMON GROUND IN CONVERSATION FOR CHILDREN ON THE AUTISM SPECTRUM

THE GREEN ZONE CONVERSATION BOOK

JOEL SHAUL, LCSW

Jessica Kingsley *Publishers*
London and Philadelphia

First published in 2015
by Jessica Kingsley Publishers
73 Collier Street
London N1 9BE, UK
and
400 Market Street, Suite 400
Philadelphia, PA 19106, USA

www.jkp.com

Library of Congress Cataloging in Publication Data
A CIP catalog record for this book is available from the Library of Congress

British Library Cataloguing in Publication Data
A CIP catalogue record for this book is available from the British Library

ISBN 978 1 84905 759 2
eISBN 978 0 85700 946 3

Printed and bound in China

CONTENTS

INTRODUCTION

What is the Green Zone?

In conversation, children with autism spectrum disorders (ASDs) often struggle to select topics of interest to others. Many have strong, narrow interests and feel compelled to introduce these subjects in conversation. In addition, children on the spectrum may be quite lacking in knowledge regarding mainstream interests and the social function of small talk.

This book provides a simple visual model to help such children experience more success in finding common ground in conversation. The "Green Zone" is a visual representation of common ground between one person (blue) and the other person (yellow) to create a "green zone" that represents the pair's shared zone of interests. The "Bright Green Zone" refers to successful conversations on topics that are primarily of interest to the *other* person, rather than oneself.

The Green Zone

Conversation Practice While Reading the Book

It is strongly recommended that you pause frequently for role play practice while using this book. The simplest way to go about this is to have children speak with you as you take on the role of the various people described in the book. Part Seven, Helping Children to Use the Green Zone Conversation Book, provides more tips about role play practice.

The Two-Person Interest Finder Pages

These two-page spreads in Part Two contain dozens of photos representing a wide range of typical interests. The Interest Finder pages enable two individuals to compare interests face to face.

The Worksheets

The worksheets in Section Two, many of which are intended to be used repeatedly, are designed to be photocopied. The Green Zone Two-Person Worksheet, which is completed by two children simultaneously, is of particular importance and should ideally be filled out repeatedly with various individuals known to the child.

THE GREEN ZONE

PART ONE

WHAT IS THE GREEN ZONE?

You enjoy thinking about your own interests.

It feels good to think about them.

You know your own favorite things better than anything else.

Let's suppose we can look inside a person's head and see what she likes to talk about.

This girl enjoys thinking about these things.

She enjoys talking about them.

Other people enjoy
thinking about what
they like.

They enjoy
thinking about their
favorite things.

They know their
favorite things better
than anything else.

This boy enjoys thinking
about these things.

He enjoys talking
about them.

15

You enjoy thinking about your own interests.

But other people are probably thinking about something else.

That's why you need to learn to talk in the Green Zone.

When you talk in the
Green Zone, that means
that you talk about things
that both you and the other
person are interested in.

It's like mixing two people's interests together to make a "new color."

Here are the two people you met earlier, and their interests. What can they talk about in the Green Zone?

19

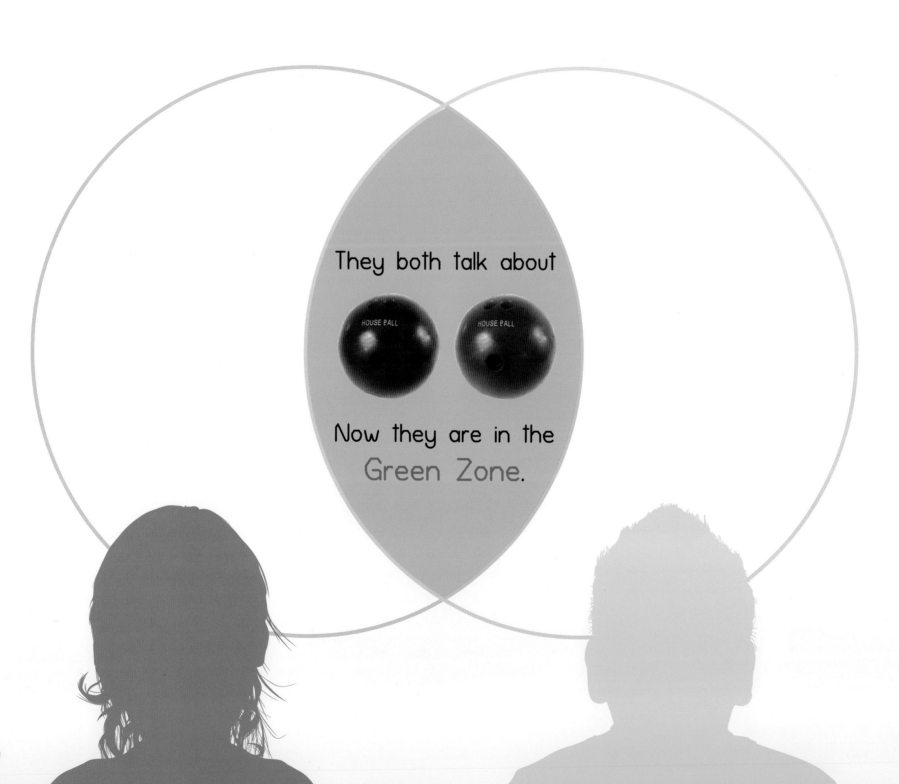

They both talk about

Now they are in the
Green Zone.

Dogs

Video games

Relatives

Army men

Today's weather

Fantasy stories

Action figures

Today's weather

Maps

Bible

Here are two new people. What should they talk about in the Green Zone?

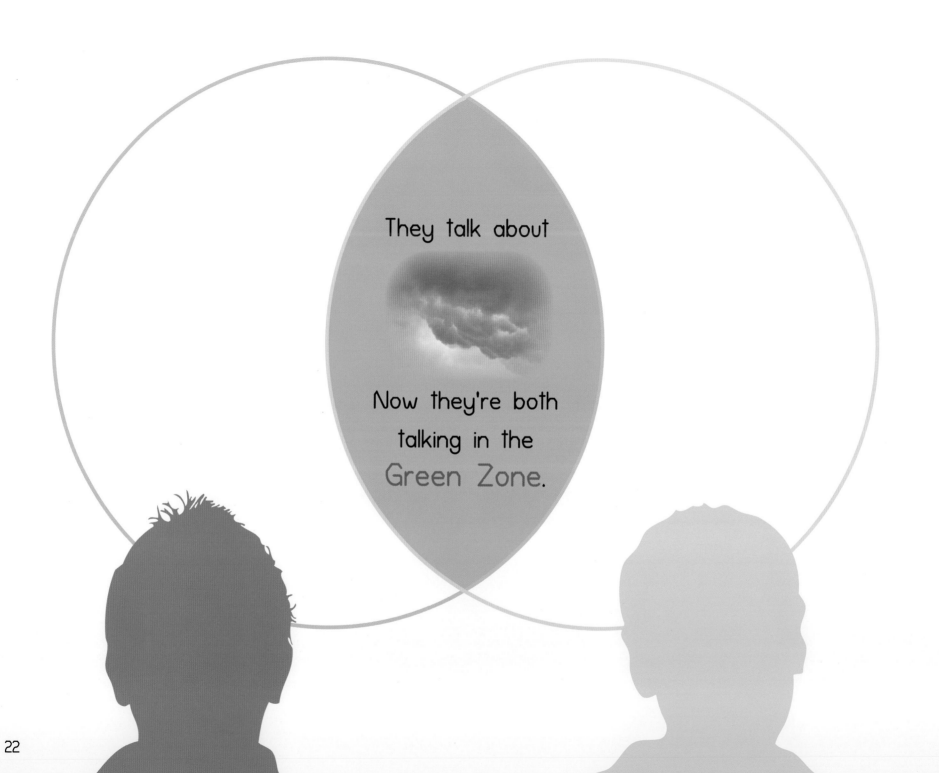

They talk about

Now they're both talking in the Green Zone.

Talking in the
Green Zone is important.

It's the main reason people
talk to each other.

It's also called "finding
things in common."

Talking in the Green Zone is kind
of like a matching game. But it's
much more than a game.

People can't just talk.
They have to try hard
to find "matches."

If people don't try really hard to get into the Green Zone, they are really just talking to themselves.

They are sort of like separate computers without the internet to connect them.

PART TWO

THE GREEN ZONE CHANGES WITH EACH NEW PERSON

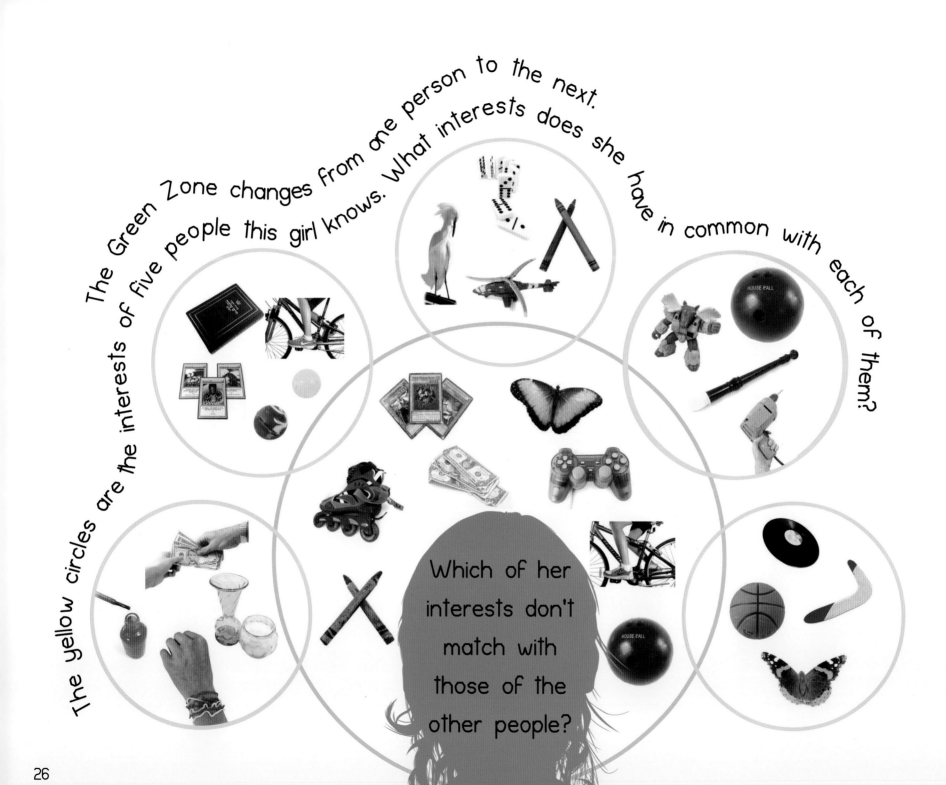

The Green Zone changes from one person to the next. What interests does she have in common with each of them?

The yellow circles are the interests of five people this girl knows.

Which of her interests don't match with those of the other people?

26

We all talk about young kid things when we are little. But the Green Zone changes as people grow up and their interests get more mature.

YOUNGER INTEREST

OLDER INTEREST

YOUNGER INTEREST

OLDER INTEREST

If children keep their younger interests as they get older, they should usually avoid talking about these things. Most other young people will have moved on in their interests.

THE TWO-PERSON INTEREST FINDER PAGES

Use these with another person to find
out how to get in the Green Zone.

COMPLIMENTS AND COMMENTS

Cool
Awesome
Interesting
That's a shame/too bad
Tell me about...
I noticed you seem to like...
You know a lot about...
You're good at...
I like how you...

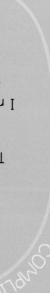  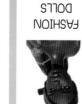     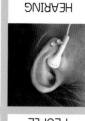

COZY TOYS · BABY DOLLS · FASHION DOLLS · DANCE · WEEKENDS · ART AND DRAWING · HEARING MUSIC · MAKING MUSIC

     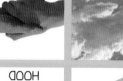

GAMES · BUILDING TOYS · SPECIAL FUN · INDOOR FUN · FANTASY WORLDS · READING, YOUNGER · MEETING PEOPLE · WEATHER

CARD GAMES · TOYS, YOUNGER · TREATS · SCHOOL · SHOPPING · HOLIDAYS COMING UP (CHRISTMAS! HANUKKAH! NEW YEARS! EASTER!) · NEIGHBOUR-HOOD

QUESTIONS

Where did you...?
When did you...?
What do you think about...?
How did you...?
How will you...?
How do you feel about...?
When did you first...?
Do you remember when...?
Who do you do that with?

WEBSITES · ONLINE VIDEOS · WARM FUN · COLD FUN · ANIMALS · RELATIVES · FAMILY

TV · CARTOONS · RADIO · BICYCLES · SWIMMING · FAMILY FRIENDS · FUNNY THINGS · FEELING GOOD ABOU...

VIDEO GAMES · MOVIES · NATURE · PLAYING SPORTS · DOGS · CATS, OTHER PETS · FRIENDS · FEELING BA... ABOUT...

THE GREEN ZONE FINDER

FEELING BAD ABOUT... — FRIENDS — CATS, OTHER PETS — DOGS — PLAYING SPORTS — NATURE — MOVIES — VIDEO GAMES

FEELING GOOD ABOUT — FUNNY THINGS — FAMILY FRIENDS — SWIMMING — BICYCLES — RADIO — CARTOONS — TV

FAMILY — RELATIVES — ANIMALS — COLD FUN — WARM FUN — ONLINE VIDEOS (VIDEOS!) — WEBSITES (WEBSITES!)

NEIGHBOUR-HOOD — HOLIDAYS COMING UP (CHRISTMAS! HANUKKAH! NEW YEARS! EASTER!) — SHOPPING — SCHOOL — TREATS — TOYS, YOUNGER — CARD GAMES

WEATHER — MEETING PEOPLE — READING, YOUNGER — FANTASY WORLDS — INDOOR FUN — SPECIAL FUN — BUILDING TOYS — GAMES

MAKING MUSIC — HEARING MUSIC — ART AND DRAWING — WEEKENDS (SATURDAY! SUNDAY!) — DANCE — FASHION DOLLS — BABY DOLLS — COZY TOYS

QUESTIONS

Where did you...?

When did you...?

What do you think about...?

How did you...?

How will you...?

How do you feel about...?

When did you first...?

Do you remember when...?

Who do you do that with?

COMPLIMENTS AND COMMENTS

Cool

Awesome

Interesting

That's a shame/too bad

Tell me about...

I noticed you seem to like...

You know a lot about...

You're good at...

I like how you...

THE GREEN ZONE INTEREST

| FACEBOOK ETC. | WATCHING SPORTS | PRETEND ACTION PLAY | READING, OLDER | CLOTHES, SHOES | RELIGION | PEOPLE WE BOTH KNOW | MY TOWN |

| MULTIPLAYER GAMES | PHONES | HAPPENING IN SCHOOL | TRAVEL, NEAR | LOOKING GOOD | ACTING | PARTIES | COLLECTING |

| COMPUTER GAMES | NEWS | MAKING PHOTOS, VIDEOS | TRAVEL, FAR | HAIR | ACTIVITIES, CLUBS | HUNTING, FISHING |

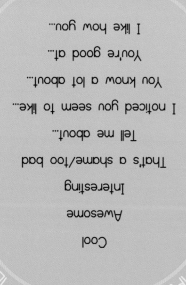

| MATH | LEARNING ON MY OWN | WORK | TOYS, OLDER AGE | GIVING | ROMANCE | OLD MEMORIES |

| SCIENCE | TEACHERS | EARNING MONEY | COOKING | HELPING | CHORES | CARING FOR OTHERS | RUNNING, WALKING |

| HISTORY | HOMEWORK | SPENDING MONEY | EATING OUT | FOOD | CARS | EXERCISE | MY FUTURE |

2025...
2035...
2045...
2055...

COMPLIMENTS AND COMMENTS

- Cool
- Awesome
- Interesting
- That's a shame/too bad
- Tell me about...
- I noticed you seem to like...
- You know a lot about...
- You're good at...
- I like how you...

QUESTIONS

- Where did you...?
- When did you...?
- What do you think about...?
- How did you...?
- How will you...?
- How do you feel about...?
- When did you first...?
- Do you remember when...?
- Who do you do that with?

THE GREEN ZONE FINDER

 MY FUTURE

 EXERCISE

CARS

FOOD

 EATING OUT

 SPENDING MONEY

 HOMEWORK

 HISTORY

 RUNNING, WALKING

CARING FOR OTHERS

CHORES

HELPING

 COOKING

EARNING MONEY

TEACHERS

 SCIENCE

 OLD MEMORIES

ROMANCE

GIVING

TOYS, OLDER AGE

 WORK

LEARNING ON MY OWN

 MATH

 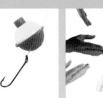 HUNTING, FISHING

ACTIVITIES, CLUBS

HAIR

TRAVEL, FAR

MAKING PHOTOS, VIDEOS

 NEWS

COMPUTER GAMES

  COLLECTING

 PARTIES

 ACTING

 LOOKING GOOD

 TRAVEL, NEAR

 HAPPENING IN SCHOOL

 PHONES

MULTIPLAYER GAMES

 MY TOWN

 PEOPLE WE BOTH KNOW

 RELIGION

 CLOTHES, SHOES

 READING, OLDER

 PRETEND ACTION PLAY

 WATCHING SPORTS

  FACEBOOK ETC.

QUESTIONS

Where did you...?
When did you...?
What do you think about...?
How did you...?
How will you...?
How do you feel about...?
When did you first...?
Do you remember when...?
Who do you do that with?

COMPLIMENTS AND COMMENTS

Cool
Awesome
Interesting
That's a shame/too bad
Tell me about...
I noticed you seem to like...
You know a lot about...
You're good at...
I like how you...

Level Zero:
The No Zone

Level One:
The Green Zone

Level Two:
The Bright Green Zone

PART THREE

THE THREE ZONES OF TALKING

LEVEL ZERO: THE NO ZONE

You are talking in
the No Zone
if you talk for a long
time about something
the other person does
not care about.

Is there anything you sometimes talk about too much?

Talking in the **No Zone** might sound really good to your own ears. But it might be painful to the other person.

Here is an example.

He keeps talking about video games! I don't even like video games.

Frank

Gina

LEVEL ONE: THE GREEN ZONE

This is when two people talk together
about something they both like.

Frank finds out that Gina likes computers as much as he does. Now they are talking at the Green Zone level.

Here is an example.

This is SO much better now! We're talking about something we BOTH like!

Frank

Gina

LEVEL TWO: THE BRIGHT GREEN ZONE

You talk about what the *other* person likes for a while, even if you don't care much about it.

Here is an example of the Bright Green Zone.

Frank finds out that Gina likes to draw.

Even though Frank does not really care much about drawing, Frank asks Gina some questions about it.

Frank acts interested.

Drawing seems important to Gina. I better ask her a couple of questions about it.

So, Gina, what are you drawing these days?

Frank

Gina

41

Gina has some good thoughts about Frank.

I like how Frank listened
when I talked about drawing.
That makes me
feel good!

42

Gina

Talking at the
No Zone
level is easy.

It's easy to talk about
what you love.

You have to really
think and listen.

Talking at the
Green Zone
level can be hard.

You search for things
the other person likes.

Then you try hard to
talk about those things.

Talking at the
Bright Green Zone
level is hardest of all.

People might tell others that you are a good listener.

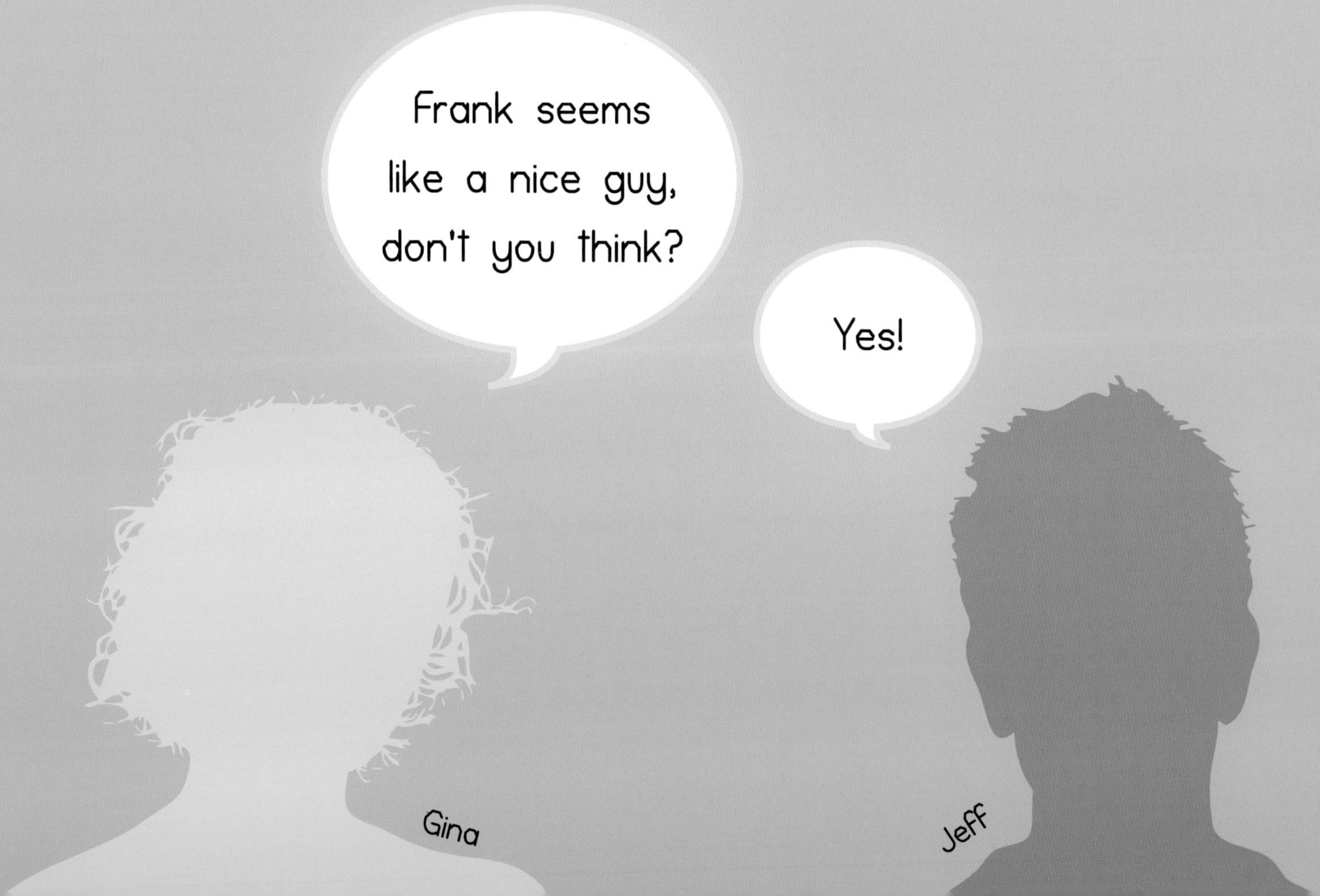

PART FOUR

TYPICAL AND UNUSUAL INTERESTS

Sometimes, people find out they are interested in the same unusual thing.

These two people are both interested in old alarm clocks.

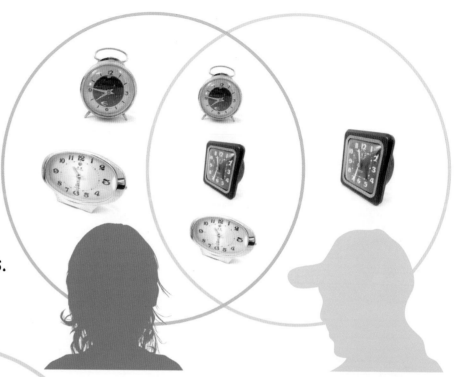

Much more often, however, people find the Green Zone with ordinary things.

These two people find they can talk together about popular shows on TV.

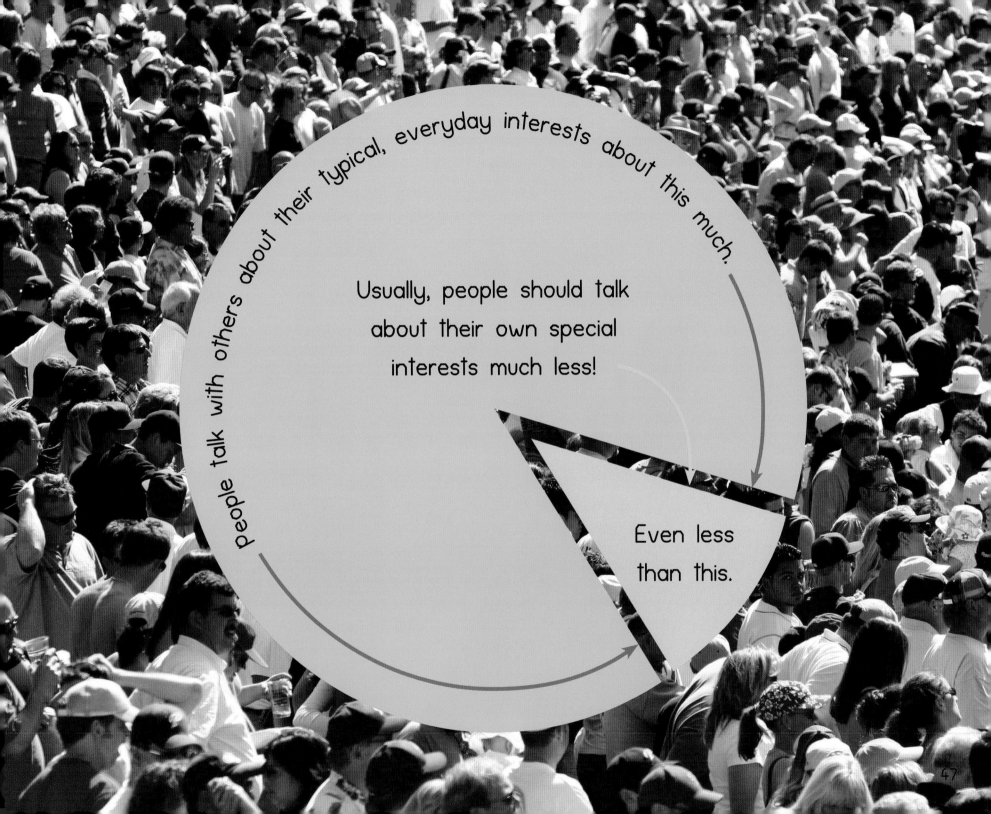

People talk with others about their typical, everyday interests about this much.

Usually, people should talk about their own special interests much less!

Even less than this.

That doesn't mean
that people's special interests
are bad. They are wonderful!

It just means that if people speak
about their special interests
too often, they won't get
into the Green Zone
as often as they
should.

People have their own thoughts while other people
are talking about their favorite things.

Read through these different possibilities.

This is quite interesting. One of my favorite topics.

I don't know much about this. Maybe I should learn more.

I can listen to this topic sometimes, but not right now.

At first, I found this kind of interesting. But after a few months, I just don't care about it much.

This is okay to hear about maybe once or twice a day.

This topic is important to this person. I will listen politely – but just for a while.

Hearing about this now, I am really thinking about how I can make it stop!

Why does this person keep talking about this? It actually makes my ears and brain hurt!

Here are some typical interests that most people can talk about together.

This is called "small talk."

Small talk is not **small**, though.

People do small talk more than any other kind of talking!

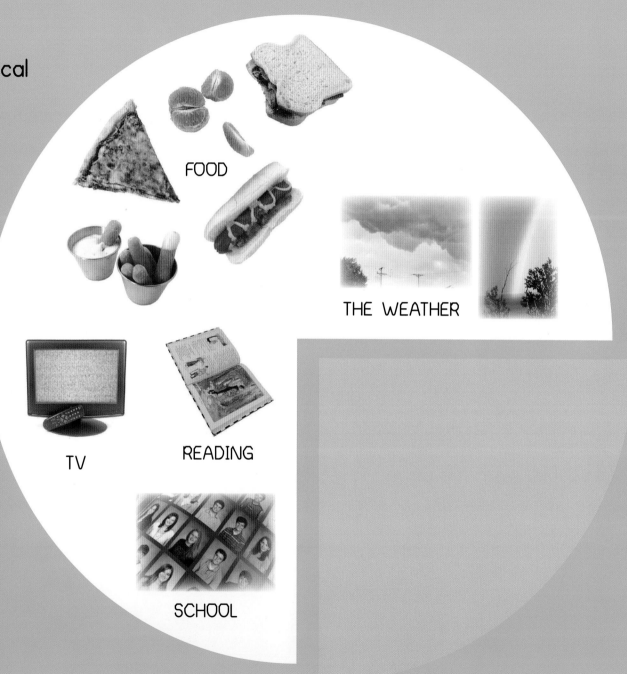

FOOD

THE WEATHER

TV

READING

SCHOOL

Here are some more examples
of typical interests that
most people can talk
about together.

HOLIDAYS
COMING

SEASONS
CHANGING

PETS

Can you think of more?

PART FIVE

QUESTIONS, COMPLIMENTS AND COMMENTS

...TO GET INTO THE GREEN ZONE AND THE BRIGHT GREEN ZONE

So, what are you doing for the holidays?

Staying home, mainly. How about you?

COMPLIMENTS: When you say you like something about someone

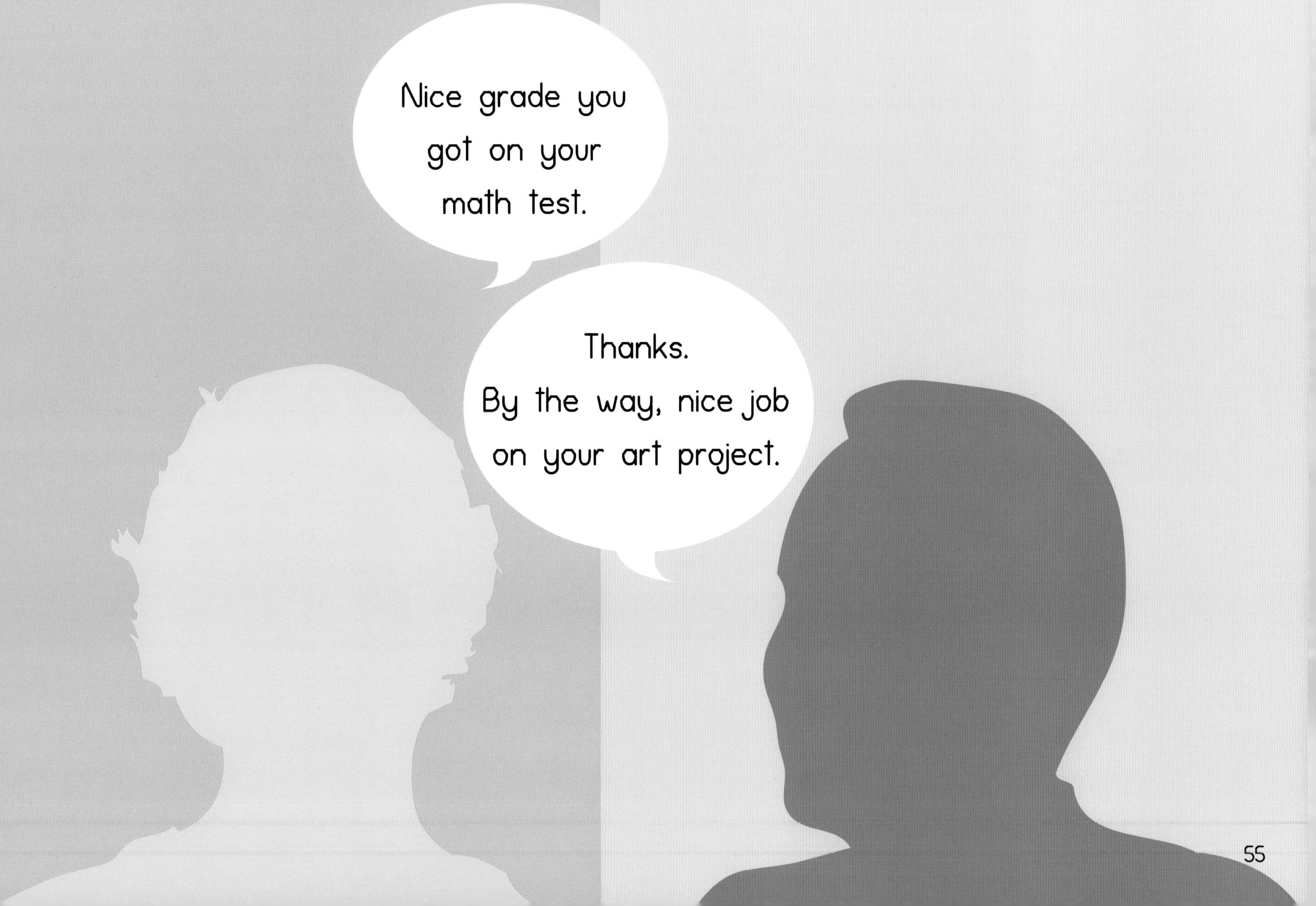

COMMENTS: Words that show you are listening and interested

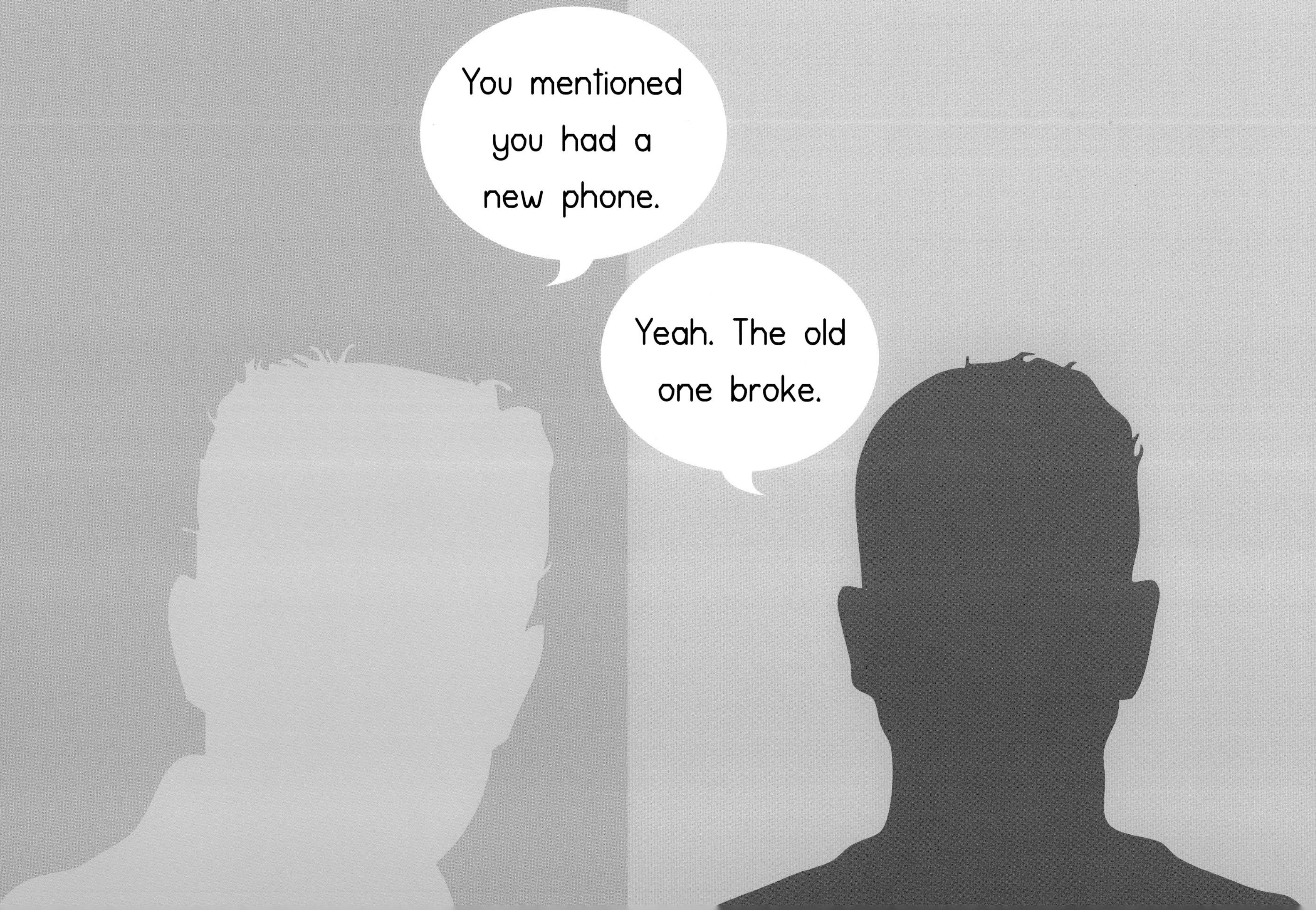

THE QUESTION/COMPLIMENT/COMMENT HELPER PAGE

- Photocopy this page to use in conversation practice with many other activities in this book.
- These aren't the only good words to say. These are just to get you started.

Questions

| Do you like...? |
| What is your favorite...? |
| What do you think about...? |
| Where did you...? |
| When did you...? |
| How did you...? |

Compliments

| Cool |
| Awesome |
| Interesting |
| I like how you... |
| You are really good at... |
| You know a lot about... |
| I like your... |

Comments

| Tell me about... |
| I noticed you seem to like... |
| I'm wondering about... |
| You said something about... |
| I'm sorry to hear that |

PART SIX

GETTING BETTER AT TALKING IN THE RIGHT ZONES

The next 13 pages show you the interests of these 13 people.

The adult with you can pretend to be each of these people.

Practice talking with each person, using everything you have learned so far.

Practice talking with
Doug

For Doug's interests that are like yours, talk with him in the Green Zone.

For his interests that are different from yours, talk with him in the Bright Green Zone.

Car his dad is working on in the garage

His knife he showed you

His two dogs

Something he likes to eat

You

Doug

Practice talking with
Tiffany

For Tiffany's interests that are like yours, talk with her in the Green Zone.

For her interests that are different from yours, talk with her in the Bright Green Zone.

Her binoculars and bird book

Places she likes to walk

You

Tiffany

Practice talking with
Mr. Max

For Mr. Max's interests that are like yours, talk with him in the Green Zone.

For his interests that are different from yours, talk with him in the Bright Green Zone.

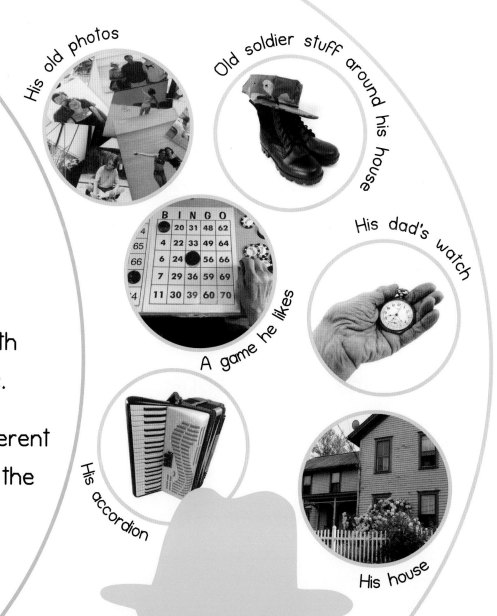

His old photos

Old soldier stuff around his house

His dad's watch

A game he likes

His house

His accordion

You

Mr. Max

Practice talking with
Maria

For Maria's interests
that are like yours, talk with
her in the Green Zone.

For her interests that are different
from yours, talk with her in the
Bright Green Zone.

Family picnics

Swings

Her dolls

Her aunt's old books

Her team

You

Maria

Practice talking with
Ron

For Ron's interests
that are like yours, talk with
him in the Green Zone.

For his interests that are different
from yours, talk with him in the
Bright Green Zone.

Boy scouts

Restaurants

Shooting baskets

His fossil collection

Running

Riding his bike

His phone

You

Ron

Practice talking with
James

For James's interests
that are like yours, talk with
him in the Green Zone.

For his interests that are different
from yours, talk with him in the
Bright Green Zone.

Toys for building

Holidays

Toys

Funny videos

Pokémon

You

James

Practice talking with
Carley

For Carley's interests
that are like yours, talk with
her in the Green Zone.

For her interests that are different
from yours, talk with her in the
Bright Green Zone.

Friends

Baking

Swimming

Babies

Treats

Hiking

Carley

You

Practice talking with
Angela

For Angela's interests that are like yours, talk with her in the Green Zone.

For her interests that are different from yours, talk with her in the Bright Green Zone.

Cool school stuff

Chess

Grandma's old things

Her school work

Her cat

You

Angela

Practice talking with
Stephanie

For Stephanie's interests
that are like yours, talk with
her in the Green Zone.

For her interests that are different
from yours, talk with her in the
Bright Green Zone.

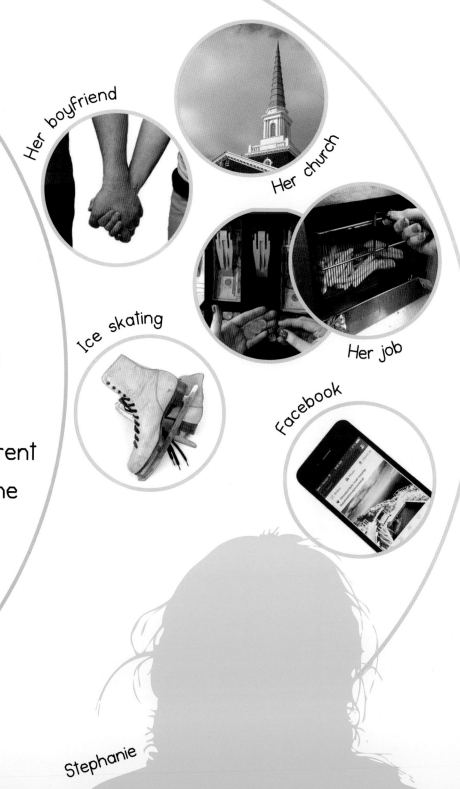

Her boyfriend

Her church

Her job

Ice skating

Facebook

You

Stephanie

Practice talking with
Carlos

For Carlos's interests
that are like yours, talk with
him in the Green Zone.

For his interests that are different
from yours, talk with him in the
Bright Green Zone.

You

Painting

His new wheelchair

Writing stories

Guitar

His fish

Hot chocolate

Carlos

Practice talking with
Adam

For Adam's interests that are like yours, talk with him in the Green Zone.

For his interests that are different from yours, talk with him in the Bright Green Zone.

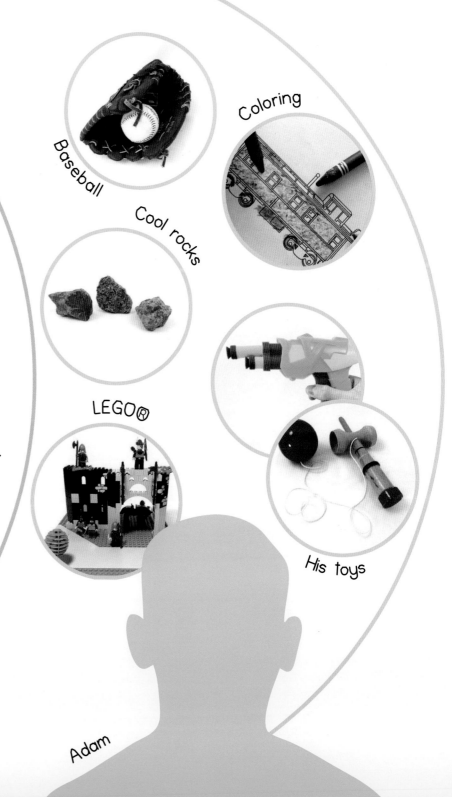

Baseball

Coloring

Cool rocks

LEGO®

His toys

You

Adam

Practice talking with
Ms. Campbell

For Ms. Campbell's interests that are like yours, talk with her in the Green Zone.

For her interests that are different from yours, talk with her in the Bright Green Zone.

Other teachers

UIZ Today

Writing a 5 ragraph.

Teaching

Salads

Knitting

Fresh Flowers

On her desk: this photo, someone's hockey trophy, fresh flowers

You

Ms. Campbell

Practice talking with

Mr. Jones

For Mr. Jones's interests that are like yours, talk with him in the Green Zone.

For his interests that are different from yours, talk with him in the Bright Green Zone.

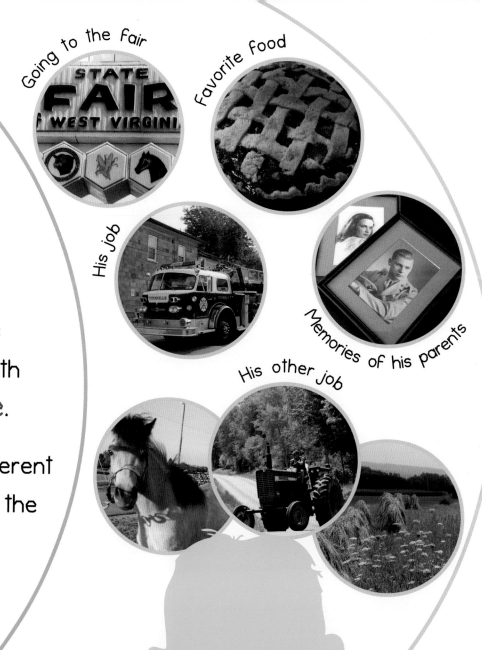

Going to the Fair

Favorite Food

His job

Memories of his parents

His other job

You

Mr. Jones

PART SEVEN

FOR ADULTS

HELPING CHILDREN TO USE THE GREEN ZONE CONVERSATION BOOK

Using The Green Zone Conversation Book and the Worksheets

A Word About Out-Loud Role Play Practice

The activities in *The Green Zone Conversation Book* are designed to set up conversation practice, directed by the adult, in these categories:

- Role play practice where the adult pretends to be one of the characters featured in the book. For example, tell the child, "Clap your hands and I will turn into Carley, a ten-year-old," and proceed.

- Conversation practice where the child and another person (adult or child) are being themselves. These are set up by the Interest Finder pages in Part Two.

- Role play practice where the child pretends to be one of the characters in the book. This is a challenging perspective-taking exercise.

While doing conversation practice in this book, shooting videos of the conversation and reviewing it with the child is a valuable teaching experience and is highly recommended.

Here is a quick visual strategy to set up role plays within the Green Zone structure. On the floor, you can create two very large, overlapping circles using paper, masking tape or chalk. Having children stand on opposite edges, challenge them to find shared interests. When they succeed, they can both step forward into the overlap portion (Green Zone).

Feel free to advance to any part of the book according to the age, needs and comprehension of the child.

Learning Activities and Worksheets for Part One: What is the Green Zone?

The Green Zone Coloring Worksheet (page 78)

This is intended to be used right after Part One: What is the Green Zone? It is a very simple sheet for younger children or for any child who really loves to color.

Learning Activities and Worksheets for Part Two: The Green Zone Changes with Each New Person

The All About Them Worksheet (page 79)

This worksheet is designed to be used before or after the introduction of the Two-Person Interest Finders in Part Two. Drawing is not mandatory, but most children will wish to include drawings.

You may have the child fill out a number of these sheets to raise awareness of the diverse interests of family members and peers.

The Two-Person Interest Finder Pages (page 29 to page 33)

There are two sets of Interest Finder pages in Part Two. Both Interest Finders reflect typical interests and are designed to be used by two individuals facing one another with the book opened up between them. The second Interest Finder also includes some photos representing older child and teen interests.

Word prompts for Questions, Compliments and Comments are provided to the left and right of the 46 picture squares. Questions, Compliments and Comments are explained in detail in Part Five.

To stimulate finding "matches," you can keep score on a piece of paper or place tokens on the table next to the book as each match is discovered.

Encourage children using the Interest Finders to talk about all of their partner's interests, not just those they share. This is introduced in Part Three as the Bright Green Zone.

Challenge children to do the matching activity with you while they are pretending to be someone they know. Show them how to stay in character while doing this. This provides a valuable perspective-taking experience.

The Green Zone Two-Person Worksheet (page 80)

The Green Zone Two-Person Worksheet is the most durable tool in this book. It is recommended that you use it often.

The two children filling out the sheet should do so simultaneously instead of taking turns. Having them work together in this manner produces a far better result. Children may need your help positioning themselves on either side of the sheet as they work together.

In the classroom, you can create a bulletin board or binder by assembling quantities of the completed Green Zone Two-Person Worksheets. This provides students with a reference when they are trying to determine what they have in common with various people they know.

CHALLENGE	SOLUTION
Children bump into each other while filling out the Green Zone Two-Person Worksheet together.	Position children facing each other across a table. Have them write sideways, diagonally, whatever works.
Child writes his interests but lacks interest in his partner's.	Reward in game-like fashion with tokens, scoring each pair of children by total of matched interests. Encourage friendly competition.
Children have difficulty finding matched interests.	Prompt them to start with "easy" interest categories: foods, holidays, video games.

Learning Activities for Part Three: The Three Zones of Talking

One reason to divide conversation styles into three ranks is to make it very clear which styles are the most advantageous. You can use the ranking system to encourage children to work hard in conversation practice.

Try saying, "When you are playing a video game, do you like to stay on the first, lowest level, or do you like to try to reach the highest level?"

Consider adding Green Zone terminology when helping children to work on conversation. Many of the words we habitually use to provide feedback to children can seem harsh and pejorative. Other expressions, like "in common," might be confusing to many children.

CONVENTIONAL CORRECTIVE LANGUAGE	GREEN ZONE LANGUAGE
"That's boring."	"Careful – that's in the No Zone."
"Find out what you have in common."	"Try to find the Green Zone with this person."
"Find out what the other person finds interesting."	"Go to the top level – the Bright Green Zone."

Learning Activities and Worksheets for Part Four: Typical and Unusual Interests

Worksheets on Typical and Unusual Interests (page 81 to page 91)

These worksheets are designed to increase the child's awareness of how his usual talking is perceived by others. It is important when working on this part to be sensitive and tactful. We don't want the child to conclude, "My interests are stupid and all I ever do is bore people." We want the child to think, "My interests are fine, but talking about them too much might not be good."

At this point in the child's learning, it can be strategic to devote some time for the child to tell others about his special interests. Other children can be coached on paying attention to the child presenting. This provides practice for all participants in the Green Zone and Bright Green Zone.

Learning Activities and Worksheets for Part Five: Questions, Compliments and Comments

Many children can find it very hard to know just what to say when they are not allowed to fall back on their own strong interests. This part shows them how to use questions, compliments and comments to help fill this void and to be more responsive to others in conversation.

When you are teaching Questions, Compliments and Comments, some children will tend to latch on to a few words and use them excessively. Encourage children to use a variety of words and phrases.

The Question/Compliment/Comment Helper Page (page 57)

It is recommended that you photocopy this page and keep it available as a reference when children are doing role play practice.

The Question/Compliment/Comment Worksheets (page 92 to page 101)

The best way to use this material is to have children read their answers out loud after having completed the worksheets.

Learning Activities for Part Six: Getting Better at Talking in the Right Zones

Children who are focused on their own interests find it very difficult to imagine what other people might be thinking about. These pages provide some examples.

Many children looking at the pictures on the pages may find that none of the pictures at all are in the Green Zone for them. Encourage children to venture into the Bright Green Zone at this point. If you like, you may reinforce this hard work by creating a "score sheet" to tally the number of points the child is "scoring" by using questions, compliments and comments in the Green Zone and Bright Green Zone categories.

Again, it is recommended that you photocopy the Question/Compliment/Comment Helper Page and keep it available as a written prompt while you are doing conversation practice with these pages.

The Another Person's Interests Drawing Sheet (page 102)

This drawing worksheet, whose graphic format mirrors the thirteen picture pages in Part Six, is designed to provide additional work for children who like to draw.

THE GREEN ZONE WORKSHEETS

Contents

THE GREEN ZONE COLORING WORKSHEET

Color this part green.

Color this part blue.

Color this part yellow.

Your name: _____

THE ALL ABOUT THEM WORKSHEET

1. On the line at the top, write down the name of someone you know (see the arrow).

2. In the four boxes below, write down four things this person likes to think and talk about.

3. Draw four small pictures showing these interests.

_____

This person

...likes to think about...

...likes to talk about...

Your name: _____

THE GREEN ZONE TWO-PERSON WORKSHEET

Person One: _____

Write some things YOU like to talk about here.

Person Two: _____

Write some things YOU like to talk about here.

When you both find things you like, write them here. Talk about these things together. Now you are in the Green Zone.

YOUR FAVORITE THINGS WORKSHEET

1. In the four boxes below, write four of your favorite things to talk about.

2. Draw four pictures showing these interests.

Your name: _____

OTHER PEOPLE'S THOUGHTS WHEN YOU ARE TALKING ABOUT YOUR FAVORITE THINGS

To get better at talking in the Green Zone, you need to know what other people are thinking and feeling while you talk.

1. In the boxes below, write down below the four things that you love to talk about the most.

2. Draw a line between the box and the thought bubble that shows what the *other person* is probably thinking when you talk.

3. Then, check your answers with the adult who is helping you.

Thoughts and feelings of someone you know named:

_____

INTEREST 1

INTEREST 2

INTEREST 3

INTEREST 4

I start to feel bored if I hear about this topic for more than half a minute.

I don't mind hearing someone talk about this topic from time to time.

Over time, I have heard about this topic so much that it is painful for me to hear about it much at this point.

This is really fascinating. I like to hear about this topic as much as possible.

82   Your name: _____

Copyright © Joel Shaul 2015

THE NO ZONE FINDER SHEET

No one is perfect! While learning how to stay in the Green Zone, everyone has to find out how they sometimes slip into the No Zone.

Try this worksheet for someone you know.

Name of one person you know:

_____

Is your favorite video game in the No Zone for this person? If so, write it here:

_____

Is your favorite YouTube video or website in the No Zone for this person? If so, write it here:

_____

Is your favorite TV show or movie in the No Zone for this person? If so, write it here:

_____

Is there anything else you love to talk about which might be in the No Zone for this person?

_____

Your name: _____

THE NO ZONE FINDER SHEET

No one is perfect! While learning how to stay in the Green Zone, everyone has to find out how they sometimes slip into the No Zone.

Try this worksheet for a few more people you know.

Name of person: _____

Is your favorite video game in the No Zone for this person? If so, write it here:

_____

If this person does not care much about your favorite website, write it here:

_____

What else do you like to talk about that this person does not care about?

_____

_____

Name of person: _____

Is your favorite video game in the No Zone for this person? If so, write it here:

_____

If this person does not care much about your favorite website, write it here:

_____

What else do you like to talk about that this person does not care about?

_____

_____

Name of person: _____

Is your favorite video game in the No Zone for this person? If so, write it here:

_____

If this person does not care much about your favorite website, write it here:

_____

What else do you like to talk about that this person does not care about?

_____

_____

Name of person: _____

Is your favorite video game in the No Zone for this person? If so, write it here:

_____

If this person does not care much about your favorite website, write it here:

_____

What else do you like to talk about that this person does not care about?

_____

_____

84   Your name: _____

THE GREEN ZONE FINDER SHEET

Your name:

_____

In the blanks below, write down some things that you and this person both like talking about:

A food you both like:

_____

A holiday you both like:

_____

An outdoor activity you both like:

_____

A person you both like:

_____

Something else you both like:

_____

Name of person you know:

_____

THE GREEN ZONE FINDER SHEET

Now try some more. Think of four people you know.

What are some things you have in common with them?

Name of person: _____

A food you both like:

_____

A holiday you both like:

_____

An outdoor activity you both like:

_____

A person you both like:

_____

Something else you both like:

_____

Name of person: _____

A food you both like:

_____

A holiday you both like:

_____

An outdoor activity you both like:

_____

A person you both like:

_____

Something else you both like:

_____

Name of person: _____

A food you both like:

_____

A holiday you both like:

_____

An outdoor activity you both like:

_____

A person you both like:

_____

Something else you both like:

_____

Name of person: _____

A food you both like:

_____

A holiday you both like:

_____

An outdoor activity you both like:

_____

A person you both like:

_____

Something else you both like:

_____

Your name: _____

THE BRIGHT GREEN ZONE FINDER SHEET

Talking in the Bright Green Zone is the highest level, and also the hardest!

1. Write down the name of one person you know:

    _____

2. Write down some things this person likes which you do NOT care about.

A TV show or movie this person likes:

_____

A computer activity this person likes:

_____

An outdoor activity this person likes:

_____

A work activity this person spends time doing:

_____

A food this person likes:

_____

Your name: _____

THE BRIGHT GREEN ZONE FINDER SHEET

Now try to find the Bright Green Zone with four more people you know.

Name of person: _____

A TV show or movie this person likes:

_____

A computer activity this person likes:

_____

An outdoor activity this person likes:

_____

A work activity this person likes:

_____

Name of person: _____

A TV show or movie this person likes:

_____

A computer activity this person likes:

_____

An outdoor activity this person likes:

_____

A work activity this person likes:

_____

Name of person: _____

A TV show or movie this person likes:

_____

A computer activity this person likes:

_____

An outdoor activity this person likes:

_____

A work activity this person likes:

_____

Name of person: _____

A TV show or movie this person likes:

_____

A computer activity this person likes:

_____

An outdoor activity this person likes:

_____

A work activity this person likes:

_____

Your name: _____

TYPICAL INTERESTS WORKSHEET

On the lines, write down as many typical interests as you can think of – that is, things that most people can talk about together.

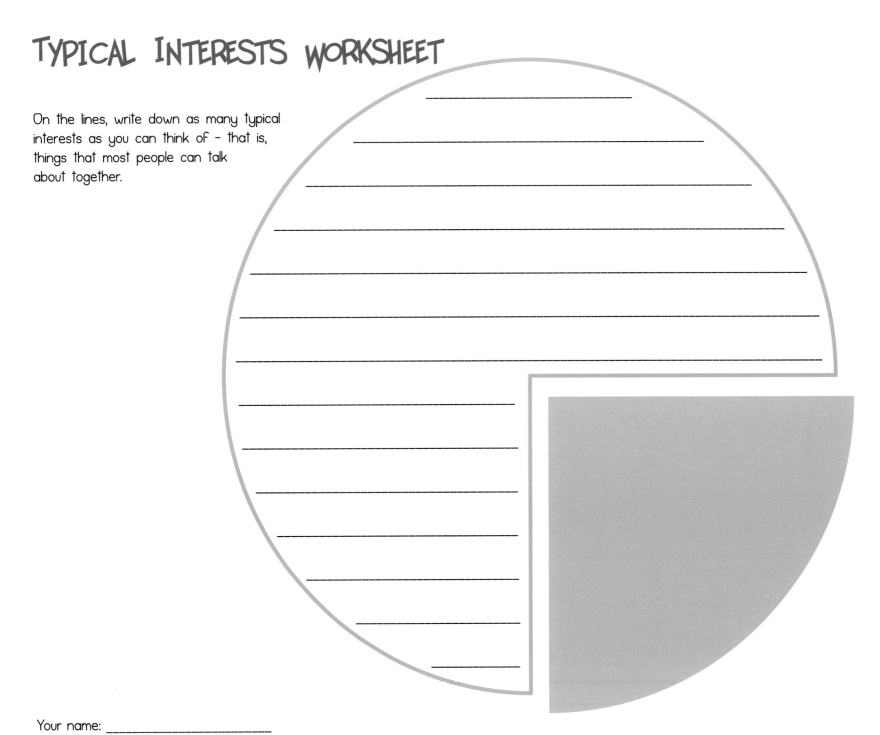

Your name: _____

89

TYPICAL AND UNUSUAL INTERESTS DRAWING SHEET

In the spaces labelled A, B, C and D, draw pictures showing typical interests you can talk about with other people.

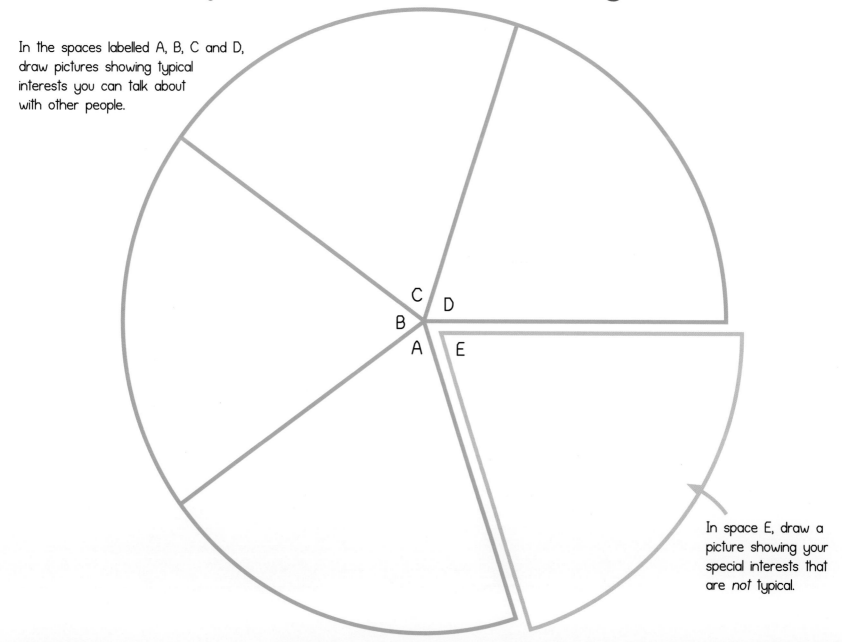

C

D

B

A

E

In space E, draw a picture showing your special interests that are *not* typical.

Your name: _____

Unusual Interests Worksheet

Here is a hard, important question:

Which special interests can you talk about less? You are allowed to ask the adult with you for help in thinking about this and writing these things down.

_____

_____

_____

_____

_____

_____

_____

_____

_____

_____

_____

_____

Your name: _____

FIND THE INTERESTS MOST PEOPLE WOULD LIKE

Here are a number of things students in school might talk about with each other.

Put a ✓ next to the ones that *most* students might find interesting, in your opinion. We did the first one for you.

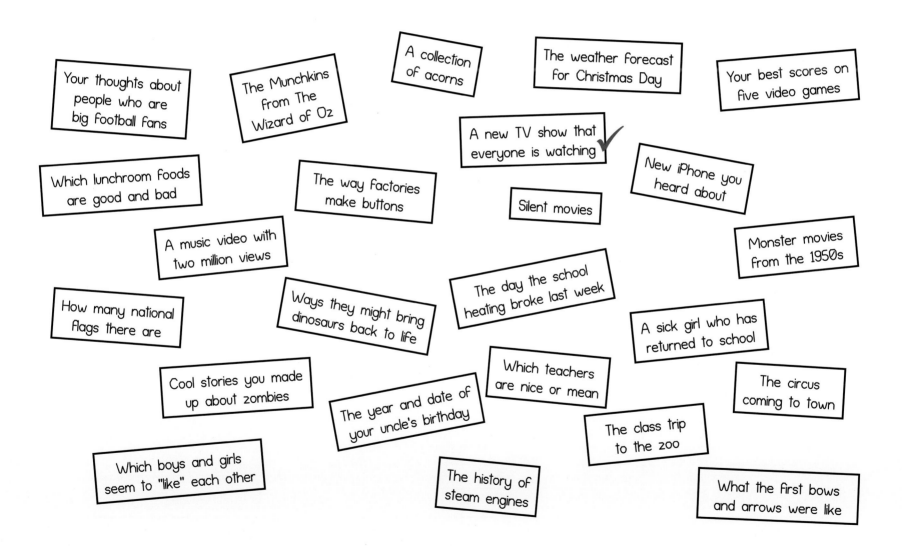

A collection of acorns

The weather forecast for Christmas Day

Your thoughts about people who are big football fans

The Munchkins from The Wizard of Oz

Your best scores on five video games

A new TV show that everyone is watching ✓

New iPhone you heard about

Which lunchroom foods are good and bad

The way factories make buttons

Silent movies

A music video with two million views

Monster movies from the 1950s

The day the school heating broke last week

How many national flags there are

Ways they might bring dinosaurs back to life

A sick girl who has returned to school

Cool stories you made up about zombies

Which teachers are nice or mean

The circus coming to town

The year and date of your uncle's birthday

The class trip to the zoo

Which boys and girls seem to "like" each other

The history of steam engines

What the first bows and arrows were like

Your name: _____

GOOD QUESTIONS PUT YOU IN THE GREEN ZONE AND BRIGHT GREEN ZONE

Good questions help you to learn more and more about the person, so you stay in the Green Zone and Bright Green Zone.

Create good questions by connecting the words and pictures.

When did you get...?

What is your favourite...?

How did you learn to...?

How did you make that...?

How do you like...?

How is your...?

What do you think about...?

Do you like...?

How long have you been...?

Are you interested in...?

How did you learn to...?

Where did you buy..?

After you are finished, you can practice by saying your questions out loud.

Your name: _____

★

PRACTICING GOOD QUESTIONS

Create good questions by connecting words on the left and right sides.

Write down the name of someone you know here.   Write down something here to finish your question.

1. _____*Mrs. Frank*_____ , what is your favorite_____*kind of candy*_____?
   [an adult]

2. _____ , what is your favorite_____?
   [an adult]

3. _____ , do you like_____?
   [a teacher]

4. _____ , what do you think about_____?
   [a boy]

5. _____ , how did you get so good at_____?
   [a girl]

6. _____ , when did you get that_____?
   [a neighbor]

7. _____ , are you interested in_____?
   [a parent]

8. _____ , how did you learn to_____?
   [a parent]

9. _____ , do you remember when we_____?
   [a parent]

After you are finished, you can practice by saying your questions out loud.

94   Your name: _____

COMPLIMENTS PUT YOU IN THE GREEN ZONE AND BRIGHT GREEN ZONE

Compliments are when you say something nice about something you see, something the other person has, or something the other person does.

Create compliments by connecting the words and pictures.

I really like your...

Cool...

Nice...

Interesting...

Awesome...

You know a lot about...

It's good how you...

I like how you...

That is quite a...

It's nice the way you...

You're getting better at...

You're good at...

Your name: _____

PRACTICING COMPLIMENTS

Create good compliments by connecting words on the left and right sides.

After you are finished, you can practice by saying your questions out loud.

Write down the name of someone you know here.   Write down something here to finish your compliment.

1. _____*Mrs. Thomas*_____ , you're good at _____*teaching*_____ .
   [an adult]

2. _____ , I like how you_____ .
   [an adult]   [something this person did]

3. _____ , that's a nice_____ .
   [a teacher]   [what he/she is wearing]

4. _____ , that was cool how you_____ .
   [a boy]   [something cool he did]

5. _____ , that was funny when you said_____ .
   [a girl]   [something funny she said]

6. _____ , that was nice when you_____ .
   [a girl]   [something nice the girl did for someone]

7. _____ , that was interesting when you talked about_____ .
   [a parent]   [something interesting they said]

8. _____ , it's good the way you_____ .
   [a parent]   [something good they do]

9. _____ , when you cook_____ , it tastes so_____ .
   [a parent]

96   Your name: _____

COMPLIMENTING PEOPLE YOU KNOW

1. Write the name of a person you can give compliments to.

2. Write down as many compliments as you can.

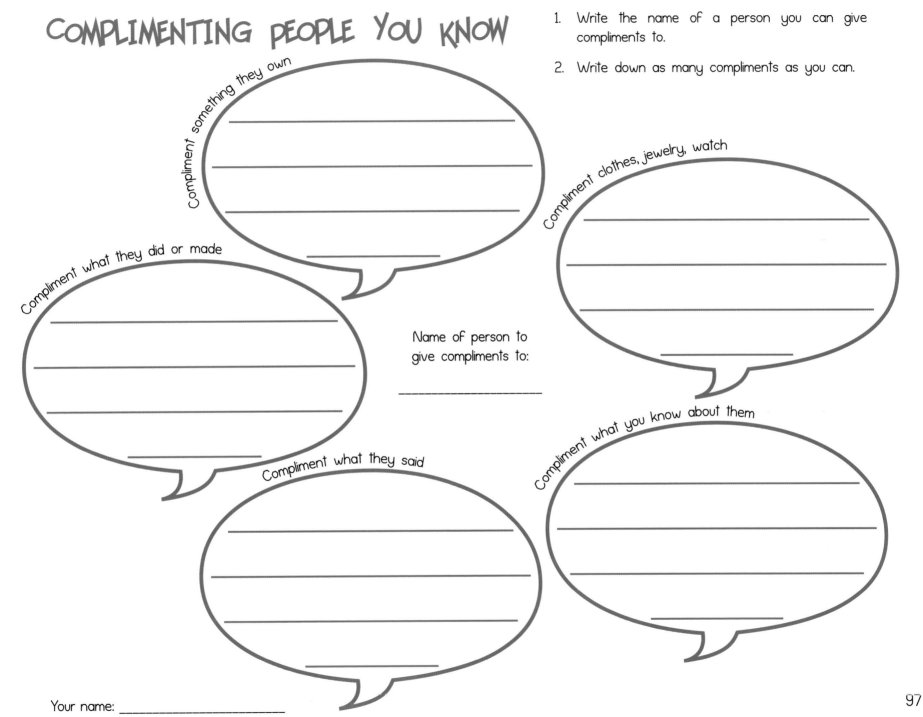

Compliment something they own

Compliment clothes, jewelry, watch

Compliment what they did or made

Compliment what you said

Name of person to give compliments to:

_____

Compliment what you know about them

Your name: _____

97

COMPLIMENTS ABOUT WHAT YOU KNOW ABOUT THE PERSON

Write the names of ten people you actually know, then a compliment to say to each of them. Use as many of the compliment words as possible. Include family members, friends, relatives, people in school. We did one example for you.

Nice

1. Mrs. Jones, you are so helpful. _____

Friendly

2. _____

Generous

3. _____

Interesting

4. _____

Funny

5. _____

Fast

6. _____

Fun

7. _____

Smart

Clever

8. _____

Hardworking

9. _____

Good at...

10. _____

Kind

98   Your name: _____

FRIENDLY COMMENTS PUT YOU IN THE GREEN ZONE AND BRIGHT GREEN ZONE

Friendly comments show other people you notice things about them.

Friendly comments help the other person to talk so you find out more about them.

Create friendly comments by drawing lines to connect words on the left with pictures on the right.

Tell me something about your...

I've never seen anything like this...

I'm wondering about your...

Please tell me more about...

You just said something about...

I've got something kind of like your...

You seem to like...

It looks like you're interested in...

I noticed you work hard at...

How long have you...

That's too bad that...

Your name: _____

PRACTICING FRIENDLY COMMENTS

Create friendly comments for someone you know. Write this person's name on the "Name of person" line. Then, complete the sentences.

Name of person:_____

1. Tell me something about your_____.

2. I've never seen anything like your_____.

3. I'm wondering about your_____.

4. Please tell me more about _____.

5. A while ago, you said something about_____.

6. I've got something kind of like your_____.

7. You seem to like_____.

8. It looks like you're interested in_____.

9. I noticed you work hard at_____.

100   Your name: _____

MAKE UP A STORY ABOUT A GIRL YOUR AGE

This pretend girl is different from you in most ways. She is like you in a few ways.

Her name: _____

She lives with_____

_____.

Her pets are_____

_____.

Her mother works as_____

_____.

Her dad is looking for a job. His job used to be_____

_____.

She is proud of her collection of_____.

Her favorite game is_____.

At school, she is good at_____.

She brings a lunch to school, which is the same almost every day:

_____.

On weekends, her favorite outdoor activity is_____

_____.

DRAW A PICTURE
OF THE GIRL

A question you could ask this girl: _____

_____

A friendly comment you could make: _____

_____

_____

Two compliments you could make to this girl: _____

_____

_____

_____

_____

Your name: _____

101

Make Up a Story About a Boy Your Age

This pretend boy is different from you in most ways. He is like you in a few ways.

His name: _____

He lives with_____

_____.

He is walking on crutches because_____

_____.

His mother volunteers at the school doing_____

_____.

His dad coaches this boy's team for this sport:_____

_____.

During lunch, you have seen him drawing pictures of_____

_____in a notebook.

He often wears T-shirts with pictures of_____

_____.

Once, he brought in the most amazing thing to show the class:

_____.

When the school cafeteria is serving_____

_____for lunch, he brings in his lunch instead.

DRAW A PICTURE
OF THE BOY

A question you could ask this boy: _____

_____

A friendly comment you could make: _____

_____

_____

Two compliments you could make to this boy: _____

_____

_____

_____

_____

Your name: _____

ANOTHER PERSON'S INTERESTS DRAWING SHEET

Draw pictures showing some things this person might like talking about.

Here are some interests of a person named:

_____

Your name: _____